CLAUSTROPHOBIC *Nightmares*

MAZES FOR ADULTS

ActivityCrusades

Published by Speedy Publishing Canada Limited

ActivityCrusades
activity books

10

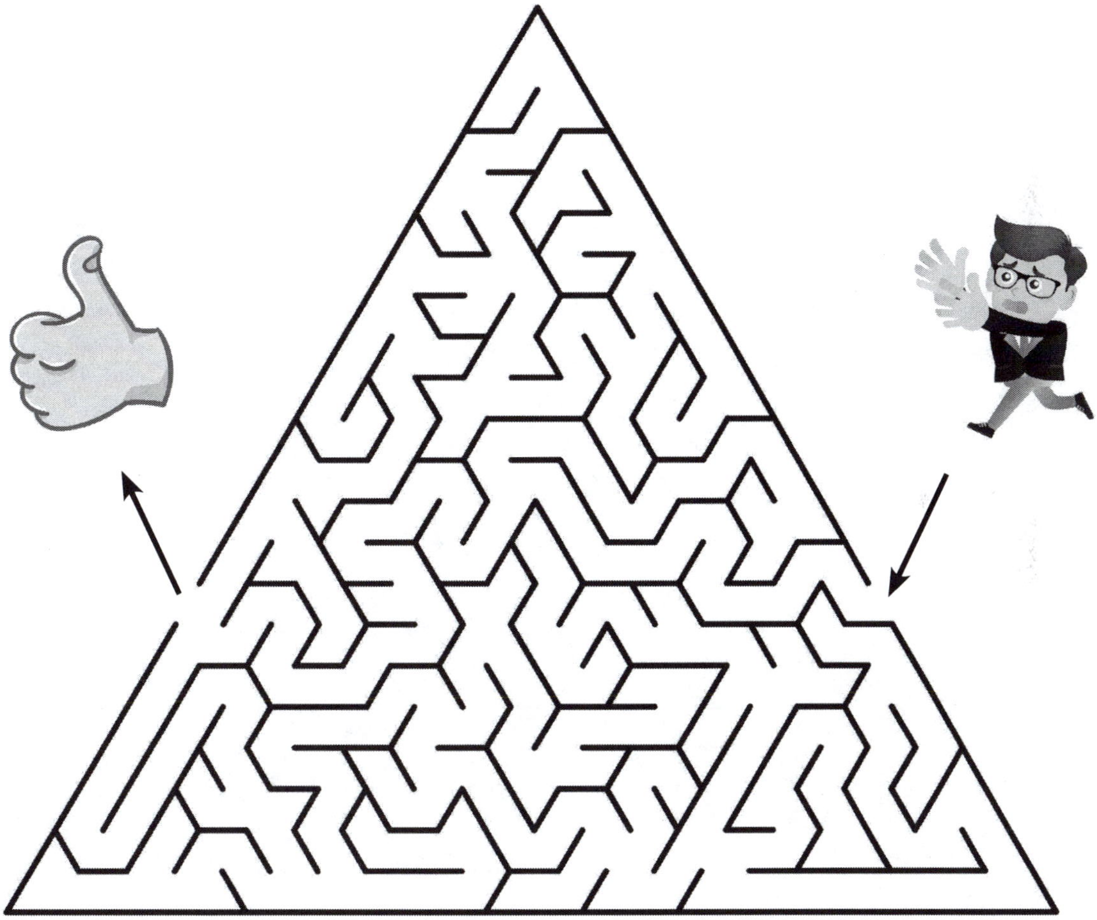

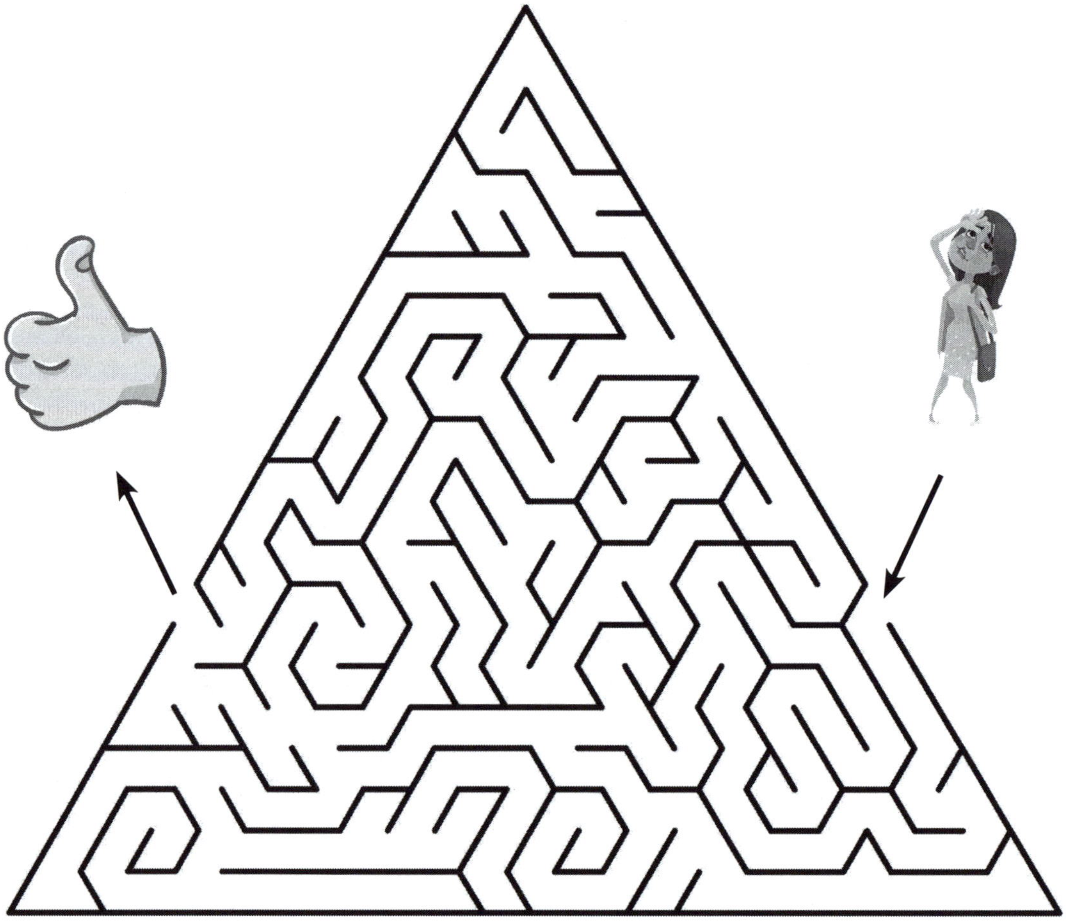

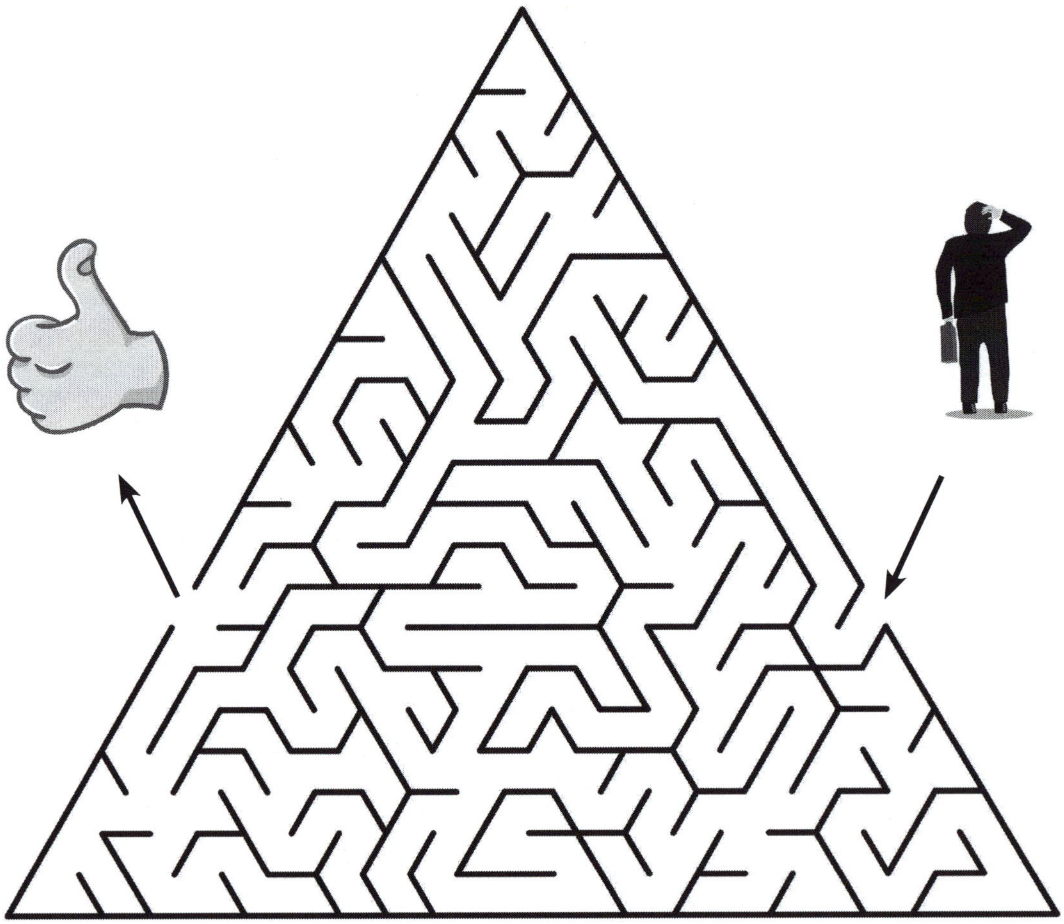

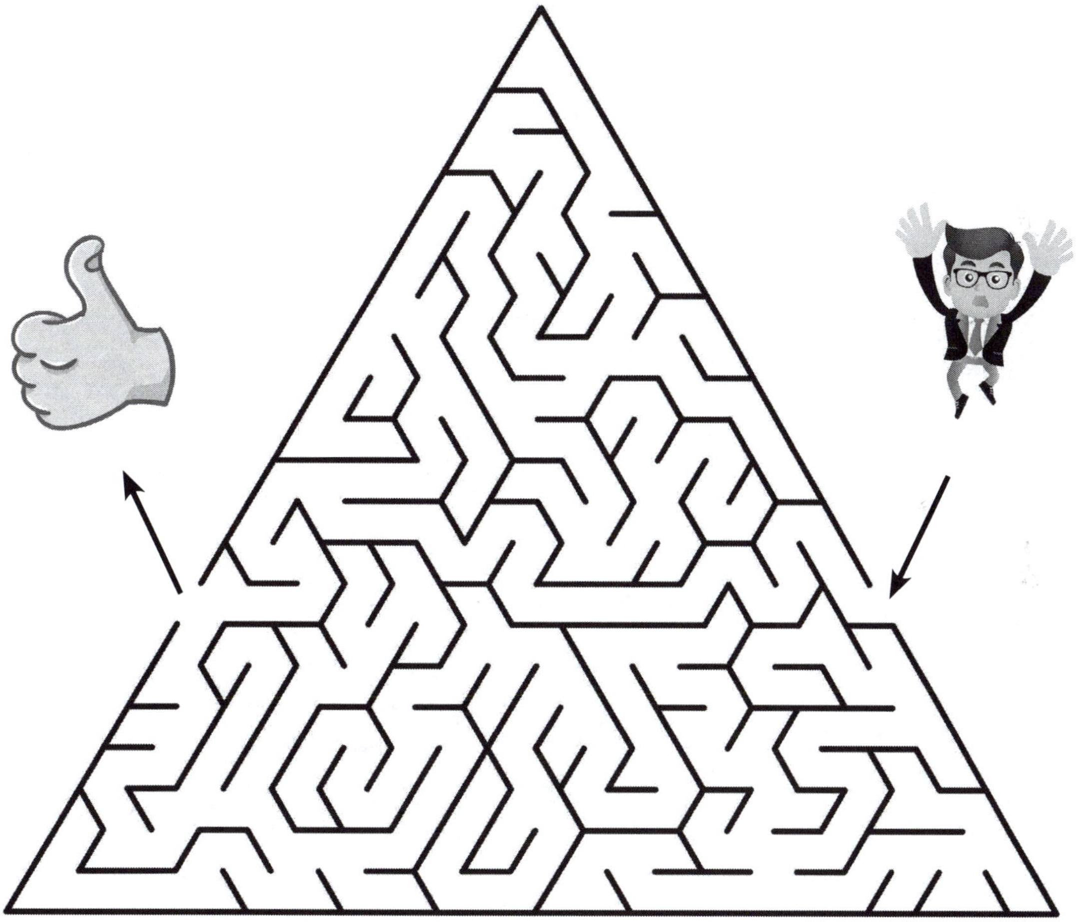

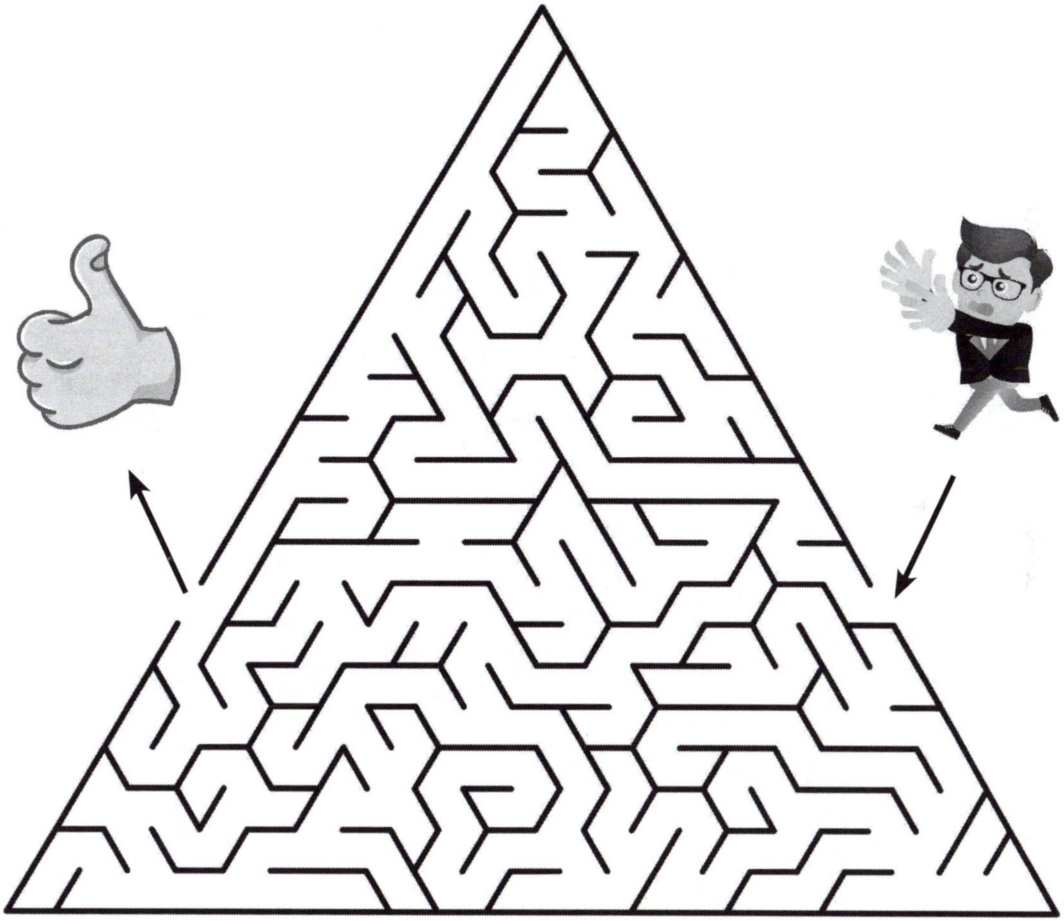

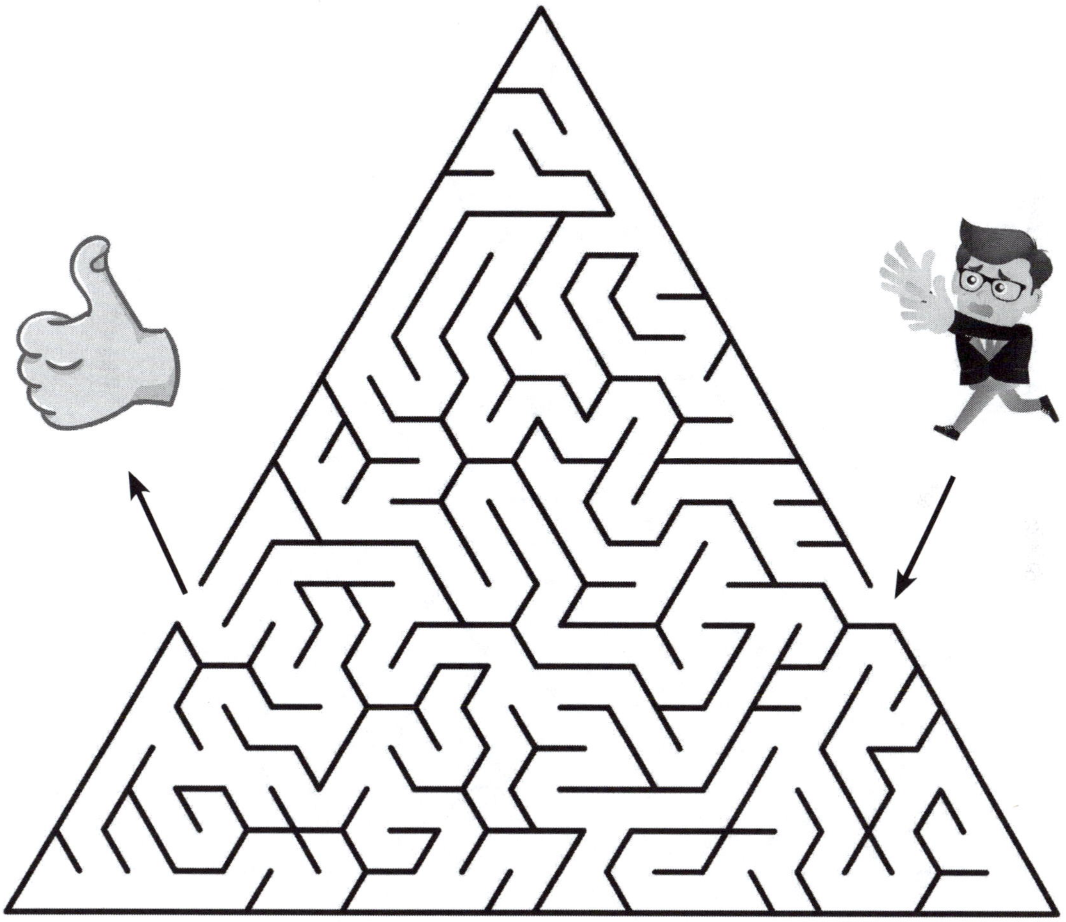

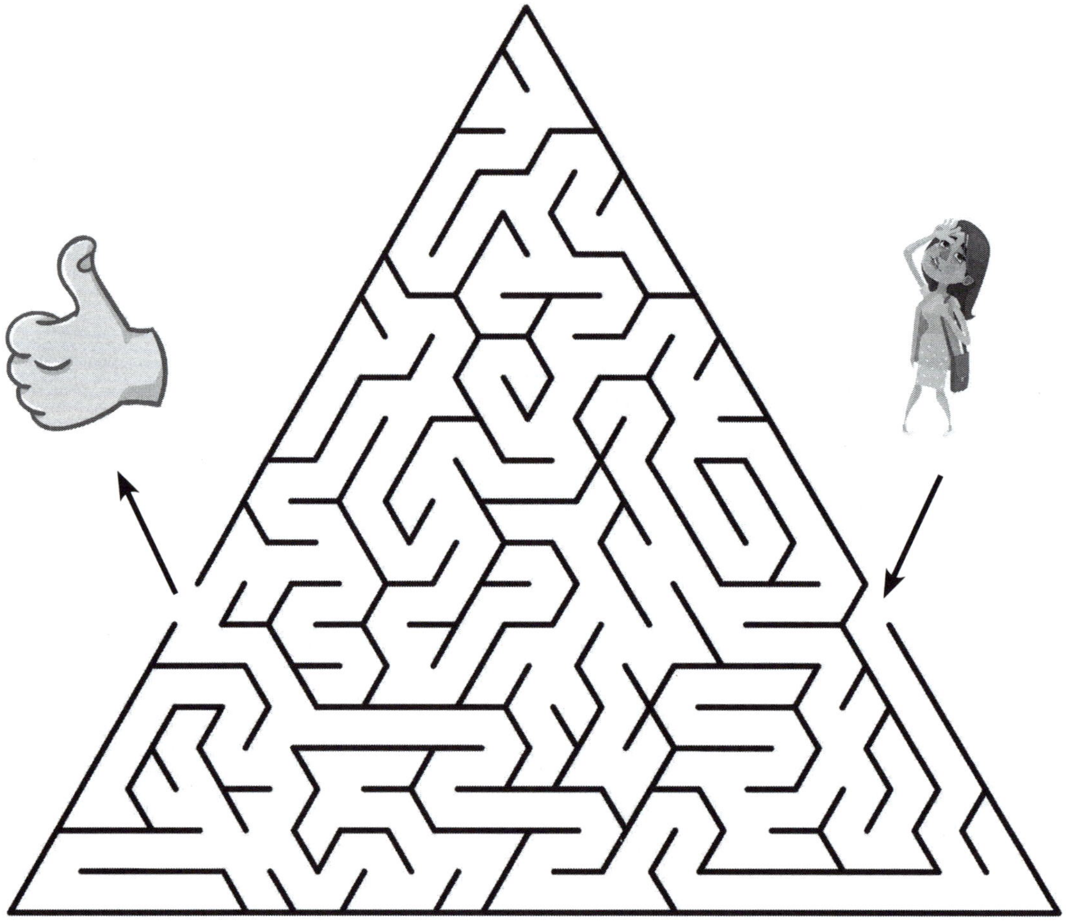

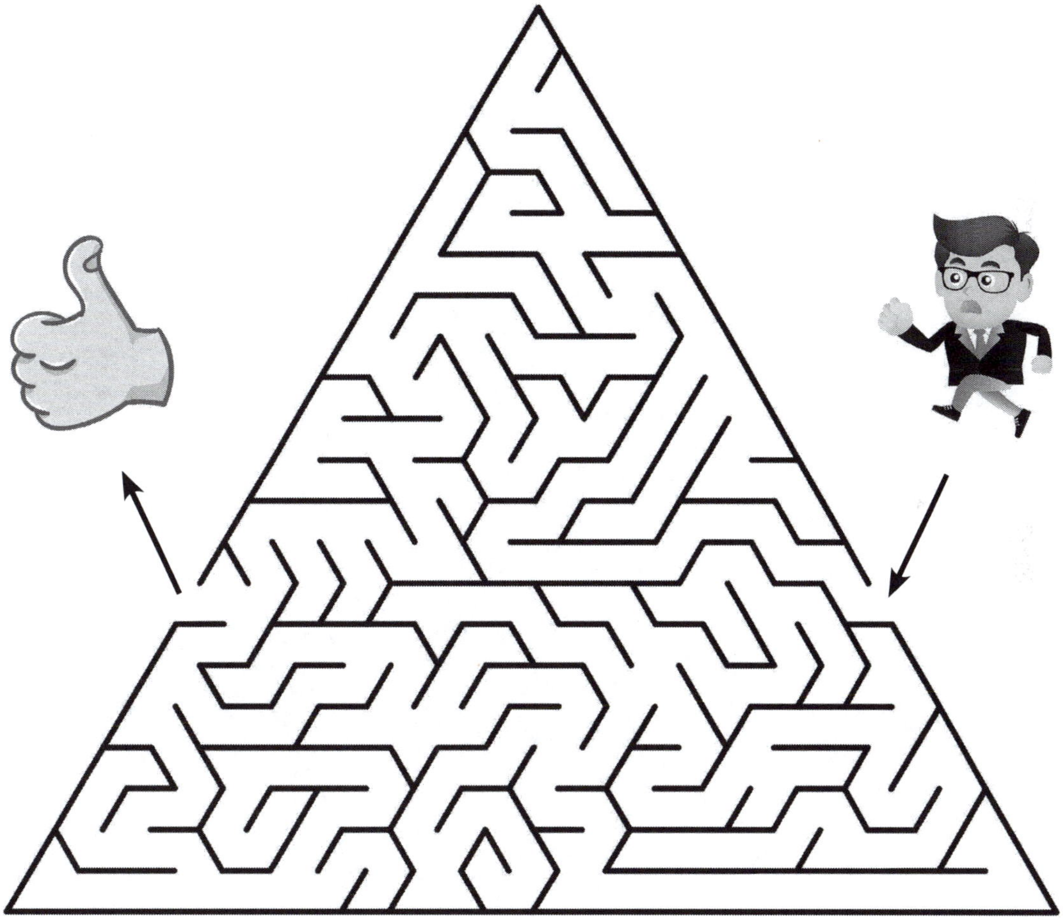

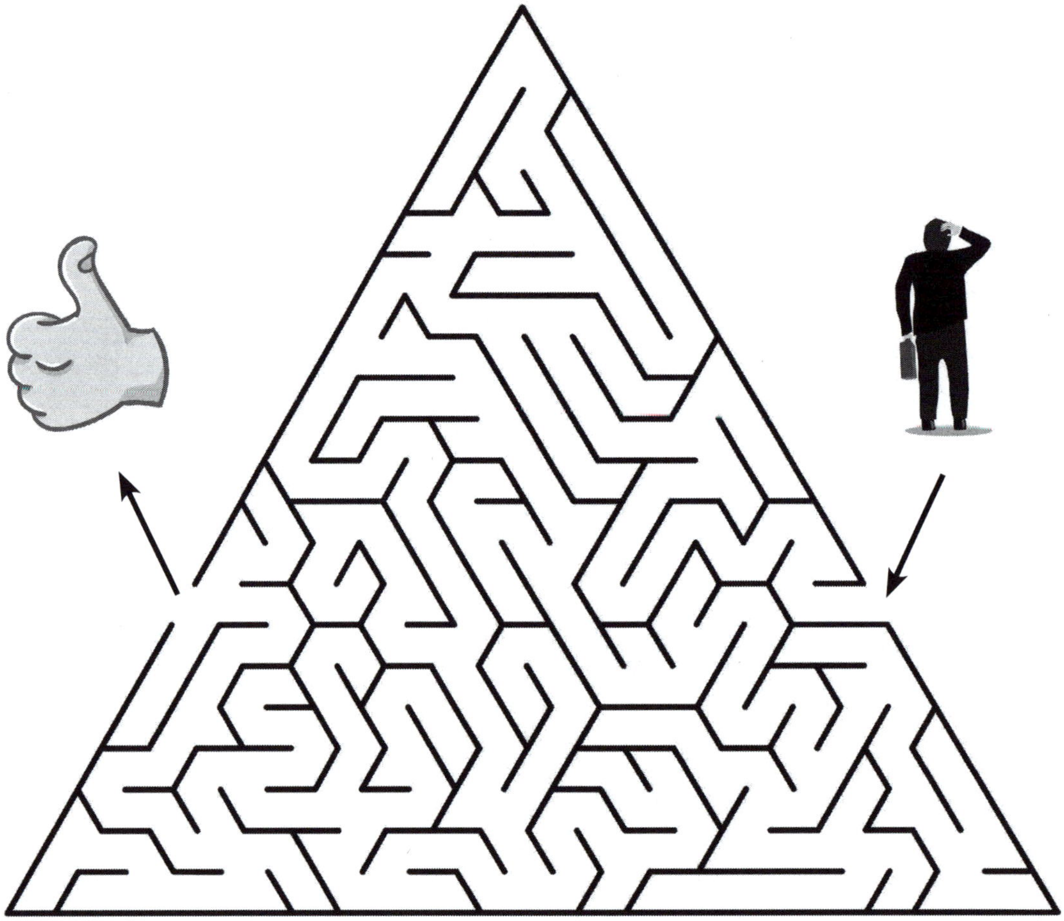

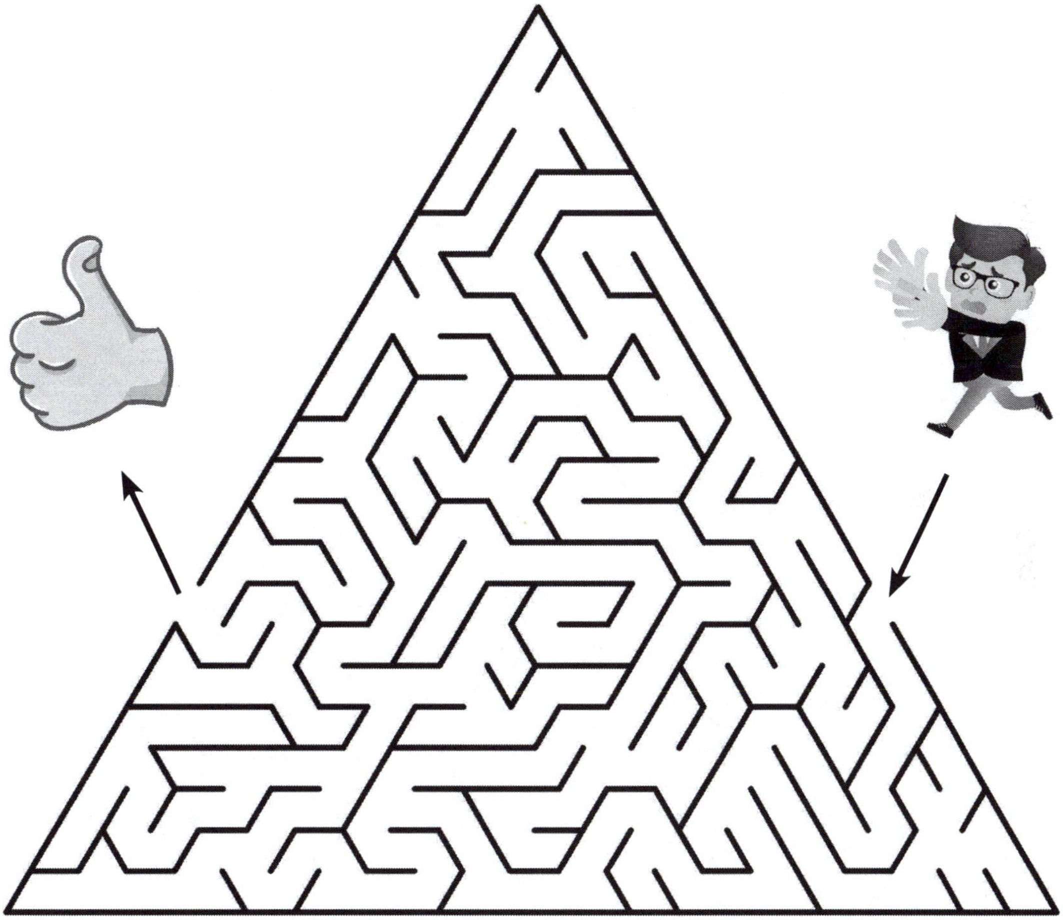

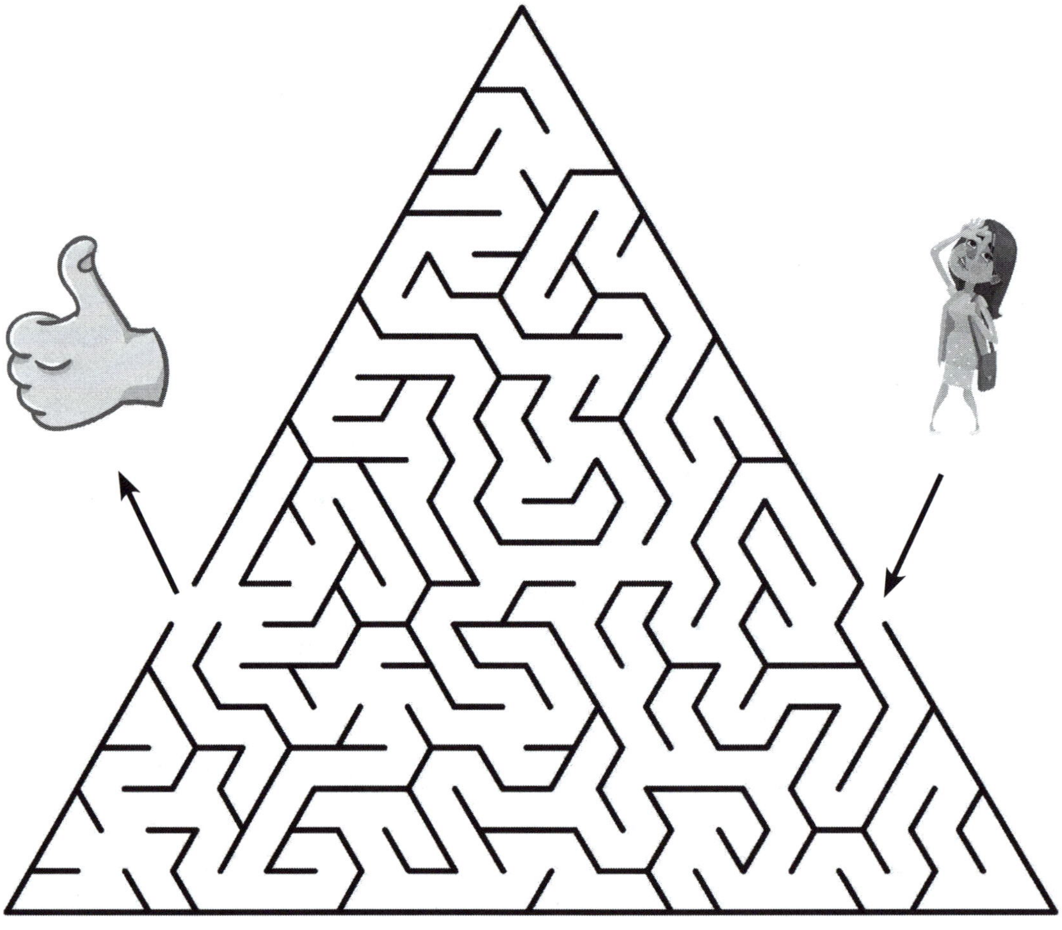

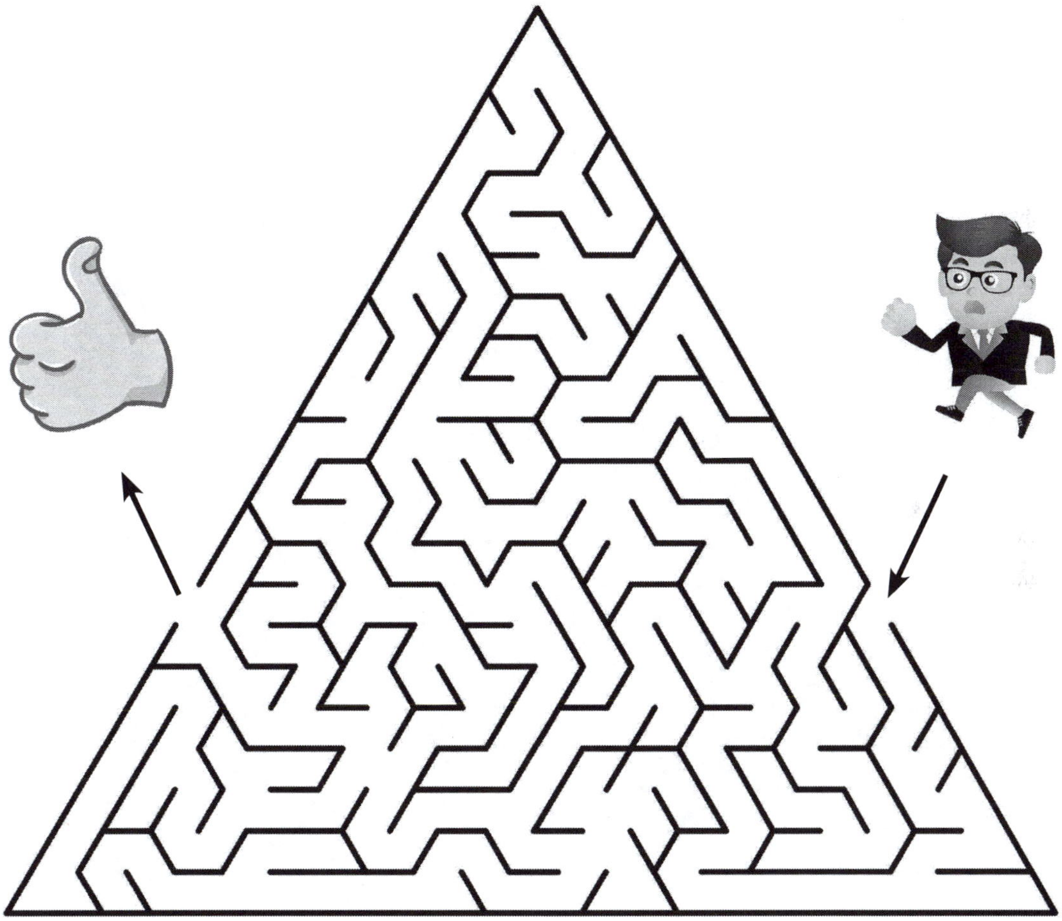

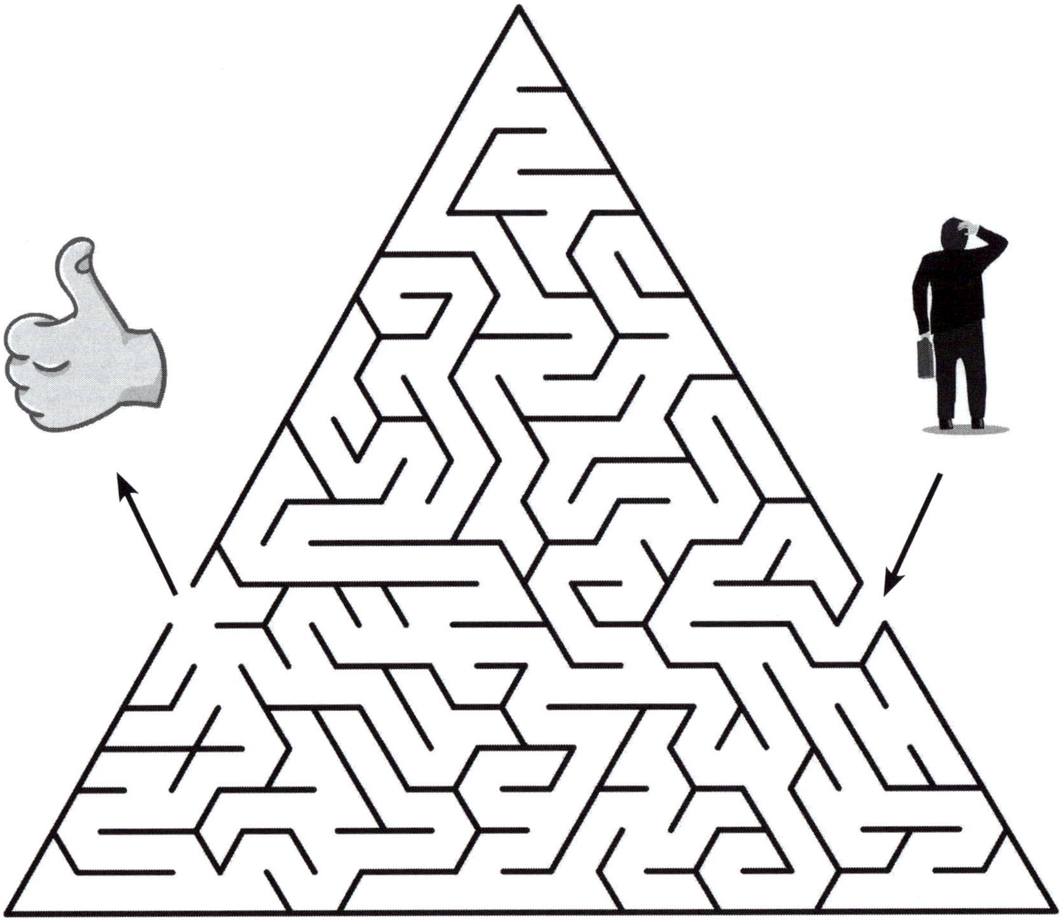

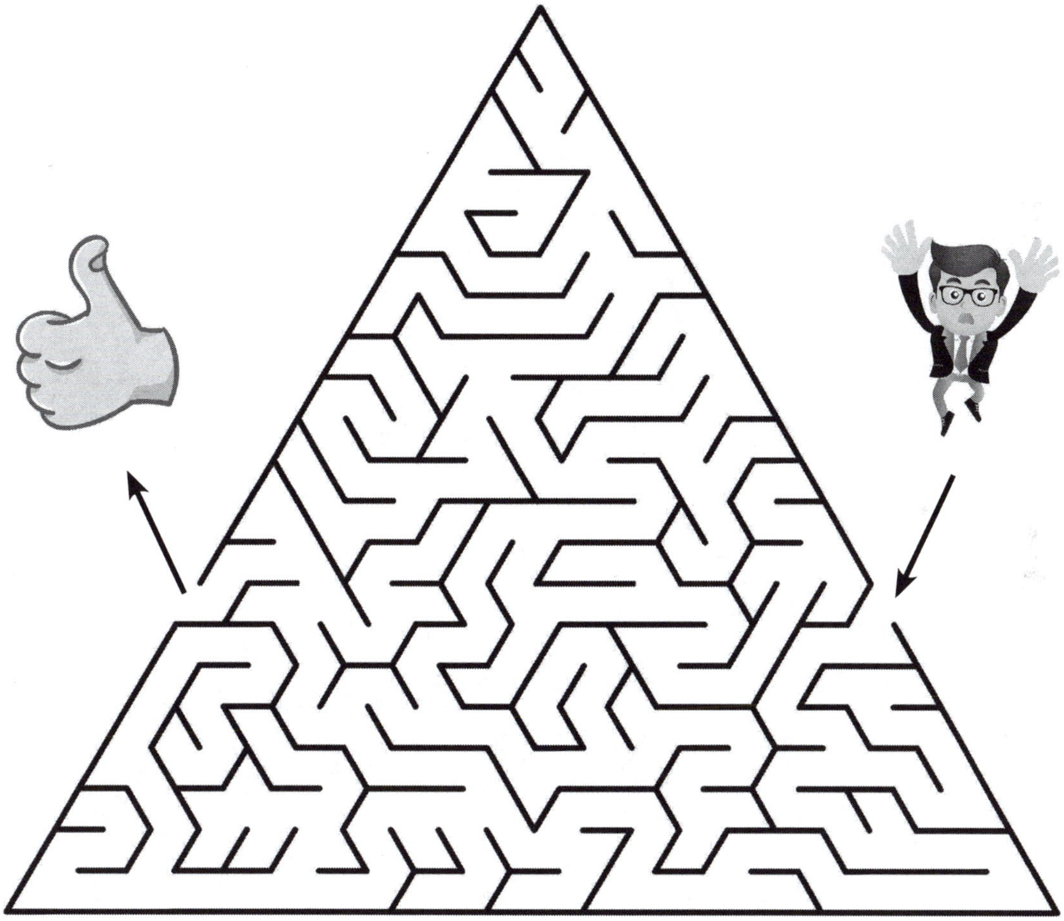

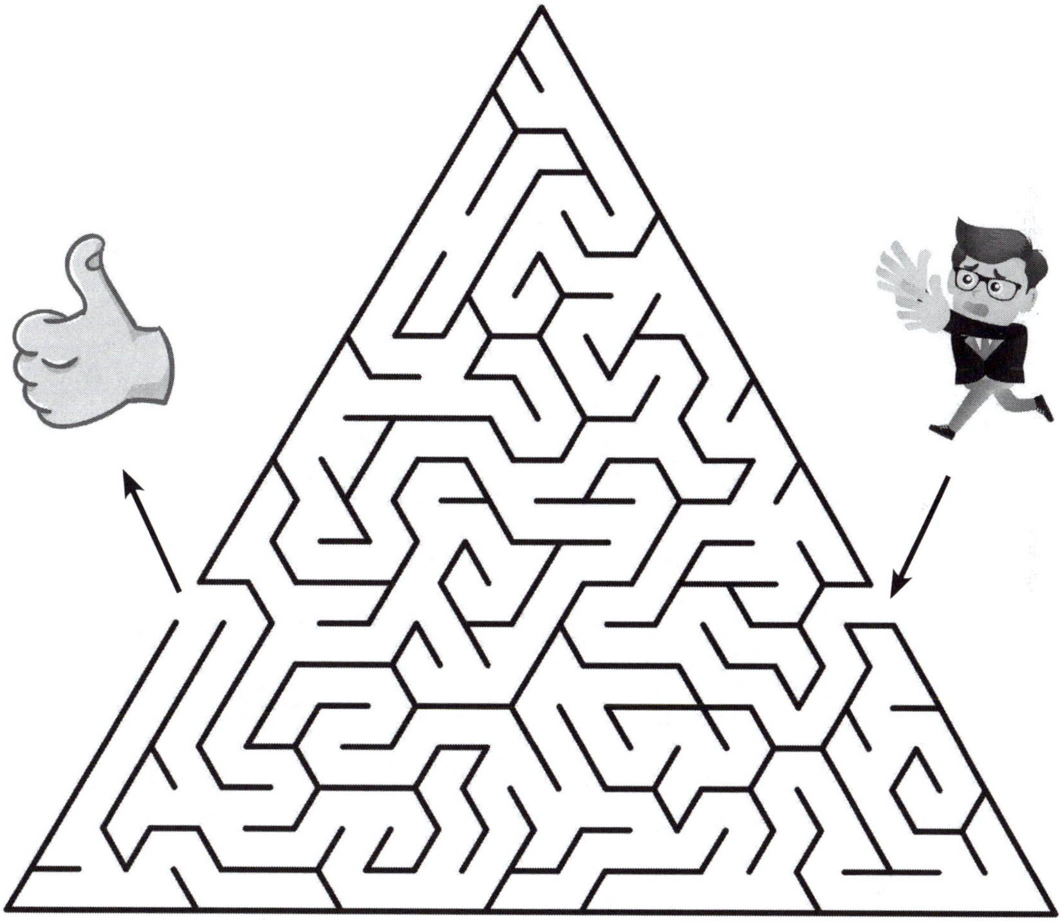

1

2

3

4

5

6

7

8

9

10

11

12

13

14

15

16

17

18

19

20

21

22

23

24

25

26

27

28

29

30

31

32

33

34

35

36

37

38

39

40

41

42

43

44

45

46

47

48

49

50

51

52

53

54

55

56

57

58

59

60

61

62

63

64

65

66

67

68

69

70

71

72

73

74

75

76

77

78

79

80

81

82

Made in the USA
Monee, IL
07 July 2026

56547356R00059